The Billionaire Tom Boi

6ColorsEnt./Billionaire Tom Boi Society 2013
Houston, Tx

FIRST EDITION

Bowker®
ISBN-13: 978-0615877396
ISBN-10: 0615877397

Interior design by Shawty Da Dayum DJ

Visit our websites ShawtyDaDayumDJ.com, 6colorsent.com, and BillionaireTomBoiSociety.com

THE

BILLIONAIRE TOM BOI

Your life's only limits are the ones you set!

SHAWTY DA DAYUM DJ

A 6Colors Ent./Billionaire Tom Boi Society Publication

Author's Preface

This book has been written to give motivation, inspiration, advice, & a good ole butt kickin' to the aspiring LGBTQ community. Before you begin reading this book, take a moment of honest self reflection. Recall your last week of watching music videos, television shows, favorite movies, or even books you read. Perhaps you stumbled across the latest Rick Ross music video release and thought "Man, Meek Mill and them boys is killin it right now! These niggas steady pullin up in Maybacks with the baddest women and money like it's nothin!" How many television shows or movies did you watch this week and sit back, mouth wide open at the success and accomplishment of people you admire and all you could say was "dang...must be nice". Now sit back and count all the people flashing on your TV screen and YouTube channels; recall how many of them are OPENLY GAY? This should piss you off and send a shocking pain so far up your spine that you can't even sleep at night. As if not being accepted in the world or being criticized daily for the "lifestyle" we lesbians "choose" to live is not enough, an absence of successful role models for us to look up to in life are just simply not there. I remember being 13 years old and so afraid of my life being destroyed just because I liked women. I could only wish to have someone to talk to about my feelings and fears, much less advice and motivation to achieve my goals or dreams in life!

What positive information, influence, road map, or self-help book was there a few years ago to help us "grow up" as lesbians, in a world that was so ready to burn us at the stake?

Today, you can't go to any city and not find at least one lesbian. It's as if a trend has broken out! Or perhaps homosexuality has been around since the beginning of time; yet ignored. Could it be that the pioneers of the community, whom have been working years towards equality, have finally succeeded? As a lesbian of 14 years, I am so proud of the barriers our gay community has broken down; yet, I acknowledge that our fight for a chance in this cold world is still NOT over. At times I fear that we are holding ourselves back from reaching the promise land because of jealousy, hatred, drama, and sabotage within our own community. Most would say, "Well, what would you expect from a room of women but a bunch of mess and drama!" But I say, if we had openly gay, successful, and inspiring mentors to look up to in the public eye besides just Ellen, Snoop, or Ru Paul, we would have no reason not to expect the best from life and behave accordingly. I feel like my family raised me well, but only to a certain extent. There are parts of myself that have grown as fierce as a lion due to the experiences both good and bad that I have learned from. I mean, where's the "lesbian guide to making a million?" There hasn't been one (that I know of) so far, so give me the opportunity to be your business partner, mentor, and/or sister so we can make some major history changing moves!

Whether we like it or not, there is a new generation of gays and lesbians emerging. Those of us 25 years old and up are the generation of fighters. As pioneers, we have loved, sacrificed, and even died so that today, in 2013, the world can no longer ignore the existence of our community. From this generation forward, lesbians have the opportunities and responsibilities to not only achieve the conquest of equality, but to also fly! We have the opportunity to take the pride of being a lesbian to the next level, where we not only declare freedom of love, but also freedom of identity and the right to live prosperously without judgment. This is such an important concept to our community, and yet, the new generation so annoyingly takes these rights for granted. Think back 5 or 10 years ago. How many 'studs' did you see, not only in America but around the world, walking around with a man's hair cut or 'double edge-up'? None of us were walking around in baggy pants and gold chains looking like Soulja Boy's lil brother, much less walking around the mall proud of new custom snapbacks and selling mixtapes. Since when did it become popular to have a 'lesbian internet radio show' or host battles for the hottest 'stud rapper'? And what the hell do lesbians know about an 'online web series' or low budget film? This culture of pride within our community has almost skyrocketed out of nowhere! This is motivating young lesbians to do something that was once crazy, like having a dream, setting a goal, and actually thinking they can become whatever they want in life. Oh yea, and doing it OPENLY GAY! A few years ago, we could only dream of a day when Da Brat would have competition! And yet here is this new generation of lesbians who see this as a normal part of their lives, half of them in big cities not ever having a taste of what it was like to grow up being told who to love, how NOT to dress, and that success would never be an option for the openly gay.

Enjoy this book. Study this book. Share this book. Feed off the positive information daily as if your success, as an openly gay individual, depends on it. As did Martin Luther King Jr., I and so many others believe and have a vision of equality for our future. We must protect our dreams, make sure to encourage one another, and most importantly, we MUST show ourselves to the world as women who benefit its' progress; not as bickering females full of drama and excuses for why we aint nothing, aint got nothing, and aint never going to be nothing! Though we are far from the end of our battle, there is no longer an excuse to say that you do not have a mentor as a lesbian.

Most of you reading this book or keeping up to date with me, through You Tube or other social media, probably laugh every time I post such crazy ideas of becoming a millionaire, much less a billionaire! What gives me the right to think it would ever be possible for a group of self-made women, much less lesbians, to roll up in a private jet or Buggatii on Lil Wayne or DJ Khaled talking about, "We here n*ggas! Let us in"? Take a moment to research the background of the top 5 people you admire most; I guarantee in most cases, they started out with little to nothing but a dream! You don't have to want millions, but whatever you want, read this book daily knowing it will help you stay motivated to never take no for an answer and fight till the death to earn what you deserve!

Introduction

Science has found that it takes 21 days to break a habit and form a new routine. This book contains 21 days of motivation, quotes, stories, and encouraging words to help you stay on top of your goals so you can run your life and stop letting it run you. You can seek all the mentors or self-help materials in the world, but until you realize that you were born with all the strength you need INSIDE of you, success will never be attained. While reading, visualize what success is to you as if you were watching yourself in a movie so you can "keep your eyes on the prize", regardless if bad things happen throughout the day. Take advantage of the "Weekly Accomplished List" so that you never forget what needs to be done each day. You should never be bored because there's always something you could be doing. Take time to reward yourself in little ways any day that you achieve every single goal on your list in a timely fashion. This way, there is no excuse to ever turn in a late assignment or forget what you were supposed to do. Don't overwhelm yourself! Set realistic daily, weekly, monthly, yearly, and 5 to 10 year goals. Use the "Notes" section to write down positive reminders that keep you smiling or motivated throughout the day. Learn to develop a positive attitude by being thankful for the great things you already have in your life and watch how more great things begin to happen. Success and accomplishment gives us all a feeling of positivity, so why would we waste time thinking about bad or negative things that happen to us? We hear it all the time, 'you are what you think'. Yet, the statement is so simple most people don't stop to think about what it really means. I hate being around people who always find something wrong with everything! Start saying positive things when they come around being negative, and watch how frustrated they get. Eventually, they will either leave your life, change positively, or they will learn not to come around you with drama or negativity. Be positive at every chance you get, and BELIEVE and KNOW that everything on this earth was put here to make sure you can do, can be, and can have EVERYTHING you want out of life.

DAY 1

Our behavior today is tomorrow's history.

Take a moment to reflect upon your current routine behaviors. For example, what type of people do you hang around on a daily basis? What is your attitude when you go to work? What's your attitude towards your future, your career, or your hobbies? How serious are you about the goals you are trying to accomplish? How often do you set aside time to work towards these things? Most people have no choice but to work 9 to 5 everyday to pay their bills on time, but the worst thing you could do is sit up and complain about the situation you are in. Today, go about your business knowing that every second you are awake is a step toward your goals. Anything you do today that is not in support of your future should be eliminated asap! The same attitudes you have today will most likely be the same in 5 years, whether you have reached success or not. I cannot express enough how important it is to act right now as if you are already who you want to be. Some type of work will always be in your life. If you aren't contributing to society, you don't deserve to reap the benefits of a luxury lifestyle. There will never be a time in your life where you sit on your ass all day. With that said, get in the habit of giving your all at work, spending time with associates who have an ambitious mindset, and any extra time perfecting the crafts that will be necessary for your future goals.

You have to believe that the things you are working towards are worth your efforts. Once you practice and perfect a behavior of meaningful efforts, the motivation you put into your daily behavior (towards tomorrow's history) will come easily.

It's not your fault that your may have been born poor or in an unfortunate situation, but it is your fault if you do not make every effort to make sure you don't live the rest of your life in a poor or unhappy position. Get up NOW and do all the things you need to, whether you want to or do not feel like it, because believe me someone else is up doing those things. Make a goal to wake up one hour earlier everyday this week and see how much more u could actually get accomplished. You see, this is a cold world so I'm not going to feed you a bunch of "smell the roses" bull crap. Life is going to be great some days but the bad days are inevitable. Like a pendulum swinging back and forth, you already know what to expect. So don't settle for what's in front of you but at the same time, don't stress yourself to death trying to control every element of an unfortunate situation. The fastest way to become a master of your life is to control how you, and only you, react to that pendulum. Take advantage of good days! When you are feeling on top of your game, make the absolute most of the time and built up positive energy within you. Know that you will have bad days and situations but don't dwell on them.

If you just can't shake the negative feelings, just take time to reflect, feel a little sorry for yourself, and then try to formulate a few steps towards resolving the problem. People waste too much time dwelling and worrying when all of their energy should be directed toward fixing the situation. Spend your bad days trying to find motivation and surround yourself with only positive thoughts and influences. Control your own mind, because it controls everything that's happening around you.

DAY 2

Wasting time trying to be someone else is a waste of the person you were born to be.

We may not admit it, but growing up we all feel this urge to be like someone we think we would like to be. There's no reason to be ashamed of this obsession, for it helps us express our inner desires and make the most of our time on earth. It becomes a problem when we envy to the point of hate and try to bring others down because of our jealousy. Or when we become so obsessed, we forget who we really wanted to be and end up feeling like we aren't good enough as we are. Loving and accepting ourselves, our faults, and obstacles is the first step to success. In doing so, we embrace the pain that comes from learning hard lessons in life that prepares us for challenges that will make us great. NEVER let anyone limit you! If you have a vision, see it through till the end. If you have a plan, follow it until it doesn't work anymore then go on to the next plan. But do this knowing that who you are and who you want to become is an exact reflection of the time and dedication you put into it. Be original and proud of what you bring to the world. Know that you aren't "trying to be" anyone else and see yourself as better than anyone could have ever imagined you could be.

DAY 3

The purpose of life is to live for a purpose! Find a purpose and give it your all!

Take a moment to reflect on why you even woke up this morning. Somewhere, someone in the world didn't get to see this day. What makes you so special that you deserve to still be breathing? Be thankful today that you even have the opportunity to have a reason to be alive. Find every reason, and GO GET IT DONE! To many times we like to get caught up in the details of life. You can sit up arguing about religion and philosophy until you're blue in the face, but from my personal experience, this is nothing but a waste of time and distracts you from your mission in life. We as humans are most happy and fulfilled when we have something we are working toward. Think about a time in your life when you worked extremely hard to accomplish something and how great you felt. What if you could have that feeling every day in your life! That's what happiness and wealth is; having total control of yourself, your life, your goals, and your dreams. It's having the freedom and limitless ability to do whatever makes you happy at any given moment. For me, happiness is being able to send my kids to the best schools and help provide the finest tools they need to succeed in their future. To me, wealth is being able to afford things like karate classes, vacations, and Chuck-E-Cheese just to see them smile. Not to mention I have the flexibility to take off of work whenever I want just to write music or take my girlfriend on a small get-a-way to Vegas. It's the ability to live in a nice neighborhood and not have to duck under the window seal to dodge bullets like I did when I was a child. It's the ability to be my own boss, work when I want, or see a Ferrari or Rolls Royce on TV and know that I could get out my chair RIGHT NOW and drive any car in the world just because I want to. I may sound materialistic, but to me, it's not about the things; it's about the ability to do or have those things and know that I can have and deserve to have access to them whenever I want. Think about all the things you would rather be doing right now than what you are doing. Are you at a dead end job when you know you would rather be on a beach? Are you in 4 year community college because your family said that's the right thing to do with your life but you'd rather be in culinary school? Did you make the junior varsity team when you feel you should have been starting quarter back on your high school varsity squad? What's your purpose and why aren't you living it right now? Start working towards that purpose and awake with that purpose on your mind every day until you achieve true happiness. You may not be doing it as big as someone else doing what you want to do right now, but that's not important. Prove only to yourself that you deserve what you want by going out and starting NOW to perfect the qualities you need to display your fullest potential in life. Write out a list of 5 things you wish to accomplish today or throughout the week. Then, take 3 post-it notes and write 3 different goals you want accomplished within 3 to 6 months or even 1 to 2 years. Put one above or next to your bed. Put the 2nd on your bathroom mirror and the 3rd somewhere that it will be with you all day like your wallet or stuck on your laptop. We'll call your 3 goals "affirmations" because you are going to "affirm" or remind your mind that this is the direction you are focused on every day. Affirm them to yourself by reading them aloud at least 2 to 3 times a day. People may look at you crazy, but so what. Ask them to support you or move around! Make them simple 1 sentence statements like "I am starting quarterback" or "I am a straight A student". Try to start them with "I am" to grind a belief within yourself so deep that no one would dare convince you of what you are 'not'. I have notes above my bed, on my bathroom mirror, and even in my wallet to keep me encouraged throughout my day. Even my children at 6 and 7 years old look themselves in the mirror as they read their daily affirmations to remind themselves of their goals.

DAY 4

You can complain about the world or conquer it.

I can't stress enough how valuable time is to success. Too many people spend way too much time complaining and feeling sorry for themselves and making excuses instead of extraordinary moves. Give it your all in the beginning and you won't have to worry about losing in the end. When you are at your lowest point in life is when your efforts count the most. If you can maintain mental focus and stay motivated, the things and people in your life can't help but to fall into place. Start today creating your own good luck. The harder you grind, the luckier you'll become. Be honest with yourself and be able to say at the end of the day that you gave your all to every second of the day. Outside of those lines, everything else will be up to the universe to make sure that your end result is indeed accomplishment. Try to be the best YOU can be for YOURSELF, not for your parents, teachers, friends, or anyone else in the world. You at your best will always be able to conquer anything life may throw your way.

DAY 5

Dress to Impress, success will come.

Contrary to popular belief, dressing as if appearance where the most important part of your day is CRUCIAL to your success in every encounter you face. Take every example you could think of, a date, a job interview, a business meeting, a concert, an album demo pitch, or buying a new car. In all of these instances, whether we want to admit it or not, the way we look and dress on a daily basis is the defining factor of how serious people will take us. When you take pride within yourself, you will put forth the most effort to show people,

and they will in turn, treat and approach you like you mean what you plan to do. Therefore, they will begin to trust that you should be presented with the best opportunities they can present to you. When you truly understand this principle, you will move beyond trying to "impress" people and it will become a natural part of expressing the inner you. This attitude will express your daily dedication to succeed and make a clear statement to the world that you expect nothing less than total success. I don't even go grocery shopping looking a mess because you never know who you'll run into. Successful people want to be around other successful people who act and look like they are "about that (success) life". Being an entrepreneur is not a goal or job; it's a lifestyle you live every single day. Make sure you're not just faking it until you make it. Live it, so we know it's real.

DAY 6

Doubt kills more dreams than fear ever will.

The biggest step you'll take on the path to success will be to overcome the fear of failure and actually make a move in the direction of your goals. Once on the path, you'll encounter what's usually referred to as beginner's luck. It's the point in the journey where everything seems to be going right and all the puzzle pieces seem to be giving you just enough motivation and encouragement to prove that your efforts will be worthwhile if you just keep moving forward. Have you ever had an unusually lucky day like this, then out of nowhere, it's as if you hit a brick wall and every step from there seems to become further and harder to reach? This is where your worst enemy (doubt) will give it all he's got! You have to do everything you can to keep faith and motivation by any means so that the distance you've reached won't be in vain. See, the fear has been overcome with the first step which is getting started. You feel all the confidence you need and no one could convince you that the goals you've set aren't possible. When you've made up your mind and set a path, stick to it but be flexible incase changes arise. Be bold, brave, and confident that any obstacles are just building blocks to your success. At this time, all your energy, expenses, time, and resources should be spent working smarter not harder. Take this time to learn all you can about what you are trying to do and how other people have been successful at it. And by all means surround yourself with positive people. To this day, I still hear my grandparents in my ear pushing me to my limits and my Uncle John always telling me how proud he was of me. Encouraging words last a lifetime. When you are in doubt, at times depression can set in and self-esteem can be lowered faster than you'll realize. You have got to keep control of your thoughts and find any way to remain calm and positive. Today, write down a few short term goals. Under each, write a step by step game plan on how you'll reach them. Next, write a Plan B next to those steps in case things change. Now you are prepared regardless if Plan A does not work out. However, it will be important that you make sure you do the things necessary to make Plan A work. Control what you can in any given situation and react calmly and intelligently to things you can't. Go get em'!!

WEEK 1 ACCOMPLISH LIST

NOTES

DAY 7

Expect less from people and demand more from yourself.

A friend of mine has quite a few friends she grew up with that seem to not be able to shake this cycle of always looking for a hand out. She called me one night complaining about yet another friend who came over to "stay a night or two" and not even a week later brought over a bag of clothes and basically moved in uninvited. How many of us have these friends, but worst of all how many of us hit a brick wall and the first thing we think is "Who can I get to bail me out of this situation?", instead of believing that we have all the strength inside to get things done. This is a dangerous mentality that has people unable to rise above their current situation. There's nothing wrong with lending a helping hand or even needing a hand every now and then. However, a successful leader is a master at having control over any threatening situation, especially proving herself when she is all she can count on. Be creative when trying to solve life's problems. If the same things you've been doing (or seeing your parents and friends do) aren't working or keep leading you to the same end result, try something different! And by all means get yourself from around people who aren't motivated to be more in life. If what you want is more, then what can you learn from them? Don't expect help from people just because they are friends or family. Be considerate that they have their own lives to account for. Take advantage of the internet and learn from those who motivate you to succeed. A few words of wisdom are worth more than a million dollar check any day, because with the right direction and determination, you'll find a million ways to make a million dollars on your own.

DAY 8

"If your dreams don't scare you, they aren't big enough." - Diddy

Close your eyes and think of something you wish you had or wish you could do like meeting a celebrity or accepting a Grammy award in front of a million people. Some of you would probably pass out on stage if it actually happened today, like right now! See, if you just want to keep being 'normal' and going through life accepting what comes, then just keep doing the little things that keep giving you little results. But if you want to accomplish your wildest dreams, you have to face your wildest fears! You have to be brave enough to do the things that all your friends are scared to do! Two years ago, I would have never imagined that I could plan, book, and actually go on my own 6 city music tour. People were like, "Come on Shawty, aint nobody from our block ever did anything like that!" I remember being 25 years old sitting with my girlfriend in my old rusty Honda saying, "Man I swear, one day I'm going to drive a Lambo and have a private jet in my music video". People have laughed at me about a lot of things I believed I could do because I could never tell them how I planned on doing it. I just knew without a doubt that I had to have a Lambo and when the time came, I was not afraid! I met a guy at a gas station one evening; I could hear my friends in the back of my mind laughing and saying I would not dare go speak to him. As I was preparing to go over to him, something came over me; an UNSTOPPABLE feeling. I mean what's the worst that could happen? He could either say yes or no! As many times in my life that I have been told no, I realized that the more crazy and insane I was about

getting something done, the faster it happened in my life! If I was thinking like an average person, I would have driven away and only been able to wonder how driving a Lambo must feel. Luckily I had a moment of insanity and have been crazy ever since! People who know me now never doubt that if I say I'm going to get something done, I DO IT! Now, whenever I get an idea or goal, I always 'over expect' and purposely try to imagine the unimaginable. At least if I fall short of the unimaginable, things will still end up pretty spectacular!

DAY 9

Speak the way you want to be heard.

It's easy to get caught up in the fun of social media and the ease of sending a text. However, never undermine the power of a person to person conversation or an intelligent email. When approaching someone you have a desire to do business with, no matter how small you may think the company or individual is, always conduct your speech as though you want to be taken serious. As much as I love to joke on Facebook or Twitter with my friends or people I don't know, I get highly irritated when people approach me or my team sounding casual and at times straight up ignorant! We aren't a Fortune 500 company, but I would expect that anyone wanting to do business with me would talk to me as thought they were serious about doing so! For example, "HeYyYy ShAwTy I wAnNa Do mUzIk WiT cHu", is the quickest way for your message or email to get over-looked and trashed! How about this email I recieved: "Aye bro wut da deal Im tryna get down wit six colors n shit peep my music I'm the hottest thang out rite now but i don't have no studio r no team n shit so i wana get wit yo team wAzZup?" Ok, I know I come off like an easily approachable person, but I'm sorry, I approach everything I do seriously and try to conduct business as though I did actually go to school to be a business owner. There are times when casual conversation may make the situation more comfortable when networking with people. However, always put your best foot forward and approach people the way you want them to come back at you. You never know whose watching or who may actually give you a shot at whatever you are trying to do. I don't mean to be an old hag, but I would like to take this time to encourage you to monitor all your posts on ALL of your social websites and keep in mind that you may miss out on opportunities because of nonsense that really has no business being public. Maybe you're the type to say, "Oh who cares, it's my life and anyone who don't like it can get the f^@#". But let me be the first to tell you that I have learned the hard way about posting "exactly what's on my mind" or pictures that were of no significance in furthering my career or goals. Besides never knowing whose looking and missing out on opportunities, another reason I keep my thoughts in my head and OFF the internet, is because you never want to give your haters ammo to use against you. Why is it their business if you're having a bad day or something didn't work out? Or why post some slick mouth trash talk when you know they are going to know it's about them? You just prove to them that they are relevant to your life and people who may have wanted to network with you may stumble upon the mess and decide not to have anything to do with you. Another thing, we all know sex sells and showing a little skin isn't always a bad thing. But allow me to take 'yo mama' side when I say, a lot of people posting half naked pics online just look thirsty, desperate, and foolish. You aren't a model just because you take a bathroom pic in your bra. You aren't the next stud stripper just because you are naked with a flat stomach and a bunch of Instagram likes. In addition, I'm still trying to figure out what is so cool about posting pics of "smoking some bomb mary jane" every 5 seconds as if it just came into style! I'm going to assume you are reading this book because you have some kind of entrepreneurial aspiration to be successful. Instead of just posting random thirsty pics for attention, why not find a cheap photographer, get your hair and nails done, find an affordable, classy, and professional outfit, then network with real models or agencies to get advice on how to build your portfolio. When you just throw yourself out there, you will most likely be denied opportunities and will attract the wrong type of attention not only for yourself, but also for lesbians and girls everywhere who are really trying to make a professional modeling career. Take some time to browse your timelines or friends lists. I guarantee the people with a page full of nothing but negative things to say, are always the first one's you find in some drama. They are probably broke and miserable and find comfort in bringing others down. I'm not perfect and I've had my share of online drama, but the more I focus and achieve my goals, the less things like beef and social popularity mean to me. The true artist, leader, or entrepreneur understands that social media is best used for promotion and new business generation, so make the most of your time online.

NOTES

DAY 10

Life doesn't give us what we need. Life almost always gives us what we deserve.

My favorite quote from Donald Trump is "The harder you work, the luckier you get." Most of us do a little work and then sit back and assume success is just a self starting roller coaster and just because we pushed the 'on' button, it's going to magically take its course. Most roller coasters take you up high into the air to build momentum before the fun begins. People get started on a project and hit a bump in the road and feel like they are at a dead end because of some unlucky circumstance. What we fail to realize is the ride can't sustain itself without constant momentum. Again, quit feeling sorry for yourself and just get use to the fact that sh*t IS GOING TO HAPPEN! If our work ethic is crap then we will continue to receive crap results. But those of us who wake up every single day keeping the momentum going in the direction of success, will enjoy the extra good luck boosts here and there. You ever wonder why it's hard to get the time or attention of wealthy or extremely successful people? You ever wonder why once an individual has made a million, they do not just retire and sit home all day smoking and watching TV? It's because their minds have gotten use to creating luck and benefiting from it, day in and day out. The momentum is motivating and good things in your life just make you want more good things. It's human nature to want all good and to do whatever we can to avoid bad. No one is going to hand the world over to you, especially if they have worked to deserve what they have. The light company doesn't just GIVE you power to your home. You give them your hard earned money so they feel you deserve to have their product. Try not paying your bill and they will surely send you a nice letter saying you don't deserve service, so they'll be sending someone out to turn your lights off. It works the other way as well. If your check from your job didn't come in on pay day, you would feel that your employer didn't deserve anymore of your time. The same goes for life and success. Tiger Woods is ranked the #1 golfer in the world but the ball doesn't just go in the hole because it doesn't like the sun. Tiger spent his whole life hitting the same balls, with the same clubs, in the same direction for hours at a time in order to have the chance to call himself the best in the world. Do you think he still practices? Yes the hell he does!! He probably practices more than people who aren't half as good as he is, which is why they'll never be as good. Put in the work, and the result can only be what you deserve. Be lazy and procrastinate, and the result will be what you deserve. The golf clubs and balls are there, but they aren't going to hit themselves. The mic and studio are there, but the music isn't going to record itself. The schools and degrees are there, but they aren't going to earn themselves. If you turn in your homework late and don't study, you deserve to fail, so stop blaming the teacher. If you don't work the overtime hours offered by your job, you don't deserve the new truck your co-worker just bought because she took the hours. Show up to practice late repeatedly, and you deserve to lose the game. The money and opportunities are in your face and that's all you need from life. Do whatever it takes to deserve them!

DAY 11

Successful people focus on results. Unsuccessful people focus on their problems.

Take today to reflect upon your thoughts and spare 10 minutes to write down everything that's on your mind. Now, read over your notes and think about all the conversations you have had throughout the week; this will help you observe where your focus truly is. Another crucial aspect to your success is how much control you are able to have over your entire life. Control begins with your thoughts and your current opinion about where your life is headed. Having the ability to focus is having total power over producing positive results in life. On the contrary, having no ability to focus usually keeps you going in circles and even making the problems you already have much bigger.

If I asked you to sit right now and make a list of all the positive results you've had over the last 7 days and then I asked you to write all the problems or obstacles distracting your focus; which list would be longer? See, having total control of your life starts with focusing all your energy to see your 'problems' or 'excuses' as extraordinary opportunities waiting to develop you into an extraordinary individual. For instance, everyone likes to walk around talking about they can't get anywhere in life because of all their haters. I always hear, "I've got a hater at work." Or, "That lady at the job interview was hating on me!" I felt bad but I couldn't help laughing when a friend of mine called me complaining that an apartment complex was "hating" and denied her application because of her criminal record. I mean, yes she was in an unfortunate situation but it's not the apartment's fault you acted a fool as a teenager. They just want to make sure their residents can live in a safe environment and I don't blame them. I believe in second chances yes, but the point I'm trying to make is that we just have to deal with the consequences of our actions and move on. She sat up depressed for several days because her "life was falling apart". I said, "No sweetheart, you are what is holding you back. Every time I see you, you're complaining about everything wrong in your life and it is usually related to your past. You've got to get up from feeling sorry for yourself and go get results by any means necessary!" In other words, focus on all the positive things that are already in your life that could help you get to where you're going. I can't say this enough, focus ONLY on those things and people that are beneficial to achieving results. You can rest assure that whether you believe you are producing results, or mainly producing problems in your life, you are absolutely right. You WILL get, do, and become exactly what you and only you believe you are. The circumstances and people chattering around you are irrelevant, therefore, the faster you realize that concept, the faster you will reach your goals. I can tell you time after time when I lived in women's' shelters, slept in my car or storage unit, got my cars re-possessed, had thoughts of suicide, and didn't know how I was going to feed my kids the next morning. However, I can tell you that even at my lowest, I always knew I had what it took to make a better life for myself. The more attention I put towards getting where I was going, the faster things changed; starting with separating myself from negative thoughts and people.

NOTES

DAY 12

Value: The size of problems that you are capable of solving.

Most self made millionaires agree that the quickest way to becoming wealthy is to provide services or products that add value and solve problems. Think about it, why would your job promote you to a higher position and pay you more money unless you are capable of solving bigger problems for them? Why should I expect to sell a million copies of any album I produce if it doesn't add value to at least a quarter million people? If I were selling toilet tissue it would be the same concept. If I expect to make millions, my product would have to add more value than the current leader in the toilet tissue market. When trying to go into business, rise in a current position, or even compete for a spot on a basketball team, you've got to be able to provide more value than the current rank holder.

Set your goals high enough to pull yourself out of your comfort zone and challenge your abilities; you'll surprise yourself and the people around you with how much you can handle. Always take advantage of an opportunity to prove your greatness. The value you bring to the table will be noticed and you'll be compensated accordingly.

Performance in Dallas, TX with Toshi of Club Elm & Pearl

On tour in Toronto with Da Brat

On tour in Vegas

Houston Splash 2013 with the crew.

DAY 13

Don't let anyone stop you from your dreams just because they gave up on theirs.

I did an interview this year and the 1st question I was asked was if I believed dreams come true and did I believe that all the work I'm doing would actually take me anywhere. I replied, "No. I don't believe dreams come true. I believe if you work hard, then what's true in your life will be so unbelievable that it will feel like you are living the dream." See, too often people put too much emphasis on dreaming and yelling 'yeah I have a dream I'm going to be this or that one day'. What those people will not admit to themselves is that the 2nd phase of a dream is going out and getting the dream accomplished. We all know someone who has worked their entire lives trying to accomplish something big but are still in the same place they started 5 years ago. You can't let seeing other people fail discourage you. Find what works for you and keep doing more of that every chance you get. You may fail, but not trying will be your biggest failure. Do basketball players just NOT shoot the ball because they are afraid they will miss? No, even professionals shoot 10 times before they actually score. If you do shoot and fail, do not focus on the failure, rather, learn from it and allow it to make you better for the next time. I don't care if it's a parent, girlfriend, husband, boss, or best friend; cut ties with anything stopping you from the direction you want to go. Jay Z said it best, "Don't listen to people; they are all afraid". Remember, fear kills more dreams than doubt ever will. You can be afraid of failing but you had better remind yourself that you should be more afraid of missing an opportunity that someone else around you took advantage of and shined.

DAY 14

Forget where you came from. It's the fastest way to get where you're going.

I'm sure I don't need to remind most of you how important leaving the past in the past is for your well being. I understand some of you have been sexually abused. I know all about being casted out because of who you are, getting evicted, or not knowing where your next meal is going to come from. Trust me, you name it, I and millions of other people in this world have been through just as much (if not more) than you. Stop looking back trying to find someone to blame for your circumstances. Own up to the role that you played in being where you are in life at this very moment because you and only you are going to be able to push yourself beyond this point. And nine times out of ten, the people you are giving so much animosity to are somewhere not even thinking about you. Karma is a universal law that is here to make sure we all get what we deserve, so let it take care of all those who have done you wrong. The only reason you should think about the past is to remind yourself of the mistakes you'll never repeat.

Last year I had an argument with a very close friend whom I really cared about. In the end, she accused me of forgetting where we came from because I had left that place in my life and she unfortunately was still there. She was the type of person that was still doing the same old things, hanging around the same old people, and living the same old dead beat life as her parents. Once I got a taste of a better life, I ran with it. I'm not saying I act boogie, arrogant, or that I just throw people under the bus because money or success has gone to my head. Anyone in my circle will tell you that I'm one of the most humble, giving individuals you'll ever meet. But at some point in my life I made the decision that I didn't want my children to have to go through anything that I could prevent and that they deserved the best of everything. From the homes we live in to the cars we drive and food we eat, why settle for the poor man's reality when the earth is full of abundance. I mean, we all go to work and work our butts off, yet more than half of Americans live below minimum wage. I realized that while I'm alive on this earth, I'm going to have to contribute my time to something or someone until the day I die. So I figured, why not work just a little bit smarter than the average man and get a lot more in return for my hard work. You see, our ancestors fought for freedom, yet our mentality is that of a slave who doesn't know he is in slavery because he doesn't see any physical chains. In society, we may have to work together to provide for one another here and there. When you are not getting paid enough to pay all your bills, can't borrow gas money from someone because you still owe them from the last time, and you have two jobs; something is seriously wrong with that picture. Yes, I've had multiple jobs, but the last year I had a job, I went to work every day with the intention that this was the last year I would ever let a job own me. If the job can't pay me what I'm worth, then I need to either boost my value by earning a degree or certification, or I need to go into business for myself. At this point in my life, I do not have a reason to go work at a job that is not offering me at least $30-40 an hour, full benefits, and freedom in my schedule. And trust me; I would still have to be doing the job just because I really WANTED to be doing it. True freedom is waking up doing what you love to do with your time. Is your time paying you or are you being paid for your time? We have got to leave what most of us have been taught behind! Your parents may not have had much and that's not your fault. There is a lot of information and many resources, such as books like mine, that are available for you to leave in the past what your parents or friends have all been doing their whole lifes. You have got to look at things differently than most people; if not, you're only going to continue being like "most people". Be patient with yourself. Most people want to get rich quick and if it doesn't come fast enough, they just quit and say, "Oh that was another money scam". Yes there are money scams out there but, most jobs these days leave you with little to survive on after paying your bills each check. Even if you are lucky to retire after holding a job for 40 years, you will only be able to retire on 40% of what you made your entire lifetime. That is the biggest scam of all time! Yet we all still get up and go to work with complaints about being unsatisfied. Let people talk and do what it is they do. If you are reading this book, you have obviously decided that you are taking time to have more, do more, and be more in life than what you've been doing. Be the BEST rapper, car salesman, or dishwasher you can be! Remember to do it with the greatness that is within you to shine, no matter who around you has failed.

WEEK 2 ACCOMPLISH LIST

NOTES

DAY 15

A man with a lot of time, rarely has any money. A man with a lot of money, rarely has time.

In other words, when you get to a point where you are so unbelievably focused and accomplished, you will notice that you don't have a lot of time for extra friends or nonsense that is not a benefit to your career or goals. Money isn't everything and should never replace the people in your life that you truly love, but how can pro boxers teach you to play football or soccer players teach you to play golf? A person who is rich has simply learned how to master the art of making money just as Tiger Woods has mastered the game of golf. When all your time is spent towards accomplishing your goals, your unreliable, negative, and unnecessary friends may find themselves outside of your life. This is a great thing and not something you should fight or be upset with! Let go of the dead weight and watch yourself fly! If you want to be a doctor, stop wasting your time with friends who want to be at the club every weekend when you know you should be focused on studying. If you want to get good at making beats, hang around people who are good at making beats! "Hanging out" is for broke people who have a lot of time and no success. I'm not saying delete your social life, but when you become so obsessed with your goals, you won't be able to eat, sleep, or breath without thinking about your next steps to victory. People who are negative or don't support your success will be annoyed by the fact that you are so focused and may even hate on you. Don't worry if you lose a friend or two, the universe will make sure to send more productive people your way.

DAY 16

Control your day, don't let it control you.

One question, how many hours in a day does Donald Trump get when he wakes up? How about Beyonce or Nicki Minaj or whoever your favorite celebrity is? Answer; 24 hours just like you and me! So what do they have that you don't, aside from a little good luck and opportunity? Answer; control over the 24 hours they are given each day. I'll tell you, no lie, about a friend of mine who's life I tried to help turn around. This woman never woke up before 11am, spent the first two and last two hours of her day smoking and eating, couldn't keep a job to save her life, and got kicked out of several family member's homes several different times. She even had the nerve to complain about her girlfriend yelling about their dirty house every day when she came home from work. She became all suicidal and tried to find every reason to blame the whole world for her problems. Her life is completely turned around now as a result of her hitting rock bottom and having no choice but to make crucial changes in her daily schedule. Studies of the average people who became millionaires by age 30 show that they wake up before 8am, don't go to bed before 10pm, rarely smoke or drink, and spend the first hour of their day reading, meditating, and preparing themselves for the day's goals. The time in your day is the most precious gift you are given when you awake. Give it ONLY to the people and the things you know are supporting your goals.

Most people's biggest challenges in making the most of their day are their stress levels and lack of sleep. As simple as it sounds, not getting enough sleep, sleeping too much, and poor health are the reason most of us feel sick and tired of being sick and tired. Perhaps if we had better stress and energy levels, we would awake earlier and be more motivated to take advantage of a few extra hours in our day.

Be patient with yourself and the frustration that may come with trying something new. Here is a little assignment to help you have the most physical and mental energy to put towards your daily routine:

1. Exercise: Force yourself to do some type of physical fitness at least 3 times a week. Everyone does not need to look like a bodybuilder, but we should all engage in some type of regular physical activity in order to promote healthy stress levels. I'm sure I do not need to go into detail how important being physically active is to your overall

well being. Start off with small activities you love doing so it does not feel like work or something you are obligated to or you will end up quitting. You do not always have to go to the biggest gym on the block. Try things like a family walk, a game of basketball, or a bike ride every other day. Start off with once a week then work your way up. Set realistic goals and don't put too much pressure on yourself about losing weight; just focus on being healthy. Keep trying new things until you find a list of things that motivate you to get out of the TV and into the beautiful world around us.

2. Keep a journal: Instead of bottling up all your worries, find a place to track how you are feeling from day to day by writing down all the things that have you stressed, happy, or feeling accomplished. Doing this will help you see firsthand what you will be dealing with that day or week. Put your worries on paper and leave them there, but try to work your way up to a full sheet of positive thoughts!
3. Eat well: I hate the word diet because people usually refer to it as if it's a formula to use only when trying to lose some quick weight. What we want to focus on here is overall wellness of mind and body. Meaning, eating healthy is not something we plan to do for a few weeks and then stop once we feel and look how we desired. The

benefits of eating healthy are more than just looking like a run-way model. Every part of our bodies from brain to muscle fibers need a certain amount of nutrients to perform at their best. Trust me, if you lay off the fast foods and sodas for ONE month, you will see a difference. I'm not a physician, but I am a former collegiate and semi-pro athlete, licensed therapist, and will be testing next month for my National Academy of Sports Medicine certification. I suggest to my clients, as well as practice, eating 6 small meals a day [every 3 to 4 hours] containing more proteins, fruits, vegetables, and water with as less carbohydrates as possible. I split my breakfast and lunch meals into 2 portions to be eaten 2 hours apart and I try not to eat after 8pm. I do not preach starvation but the less bulky meals you eat, the lighter and more energy you will feel.

4. Massage and stretching: Getting a professional massage is one of the best things you can do for your body. Drinking plenty of water and stretching throughout releases many toxins from your body and helps it recover quicker from stress and even injuries. Massage also helps the body's circulatory system and helps to keep your hormones in balance. This process reduces stress and keeps your mood feeling more positive. No scientific explanation need, massage is just one of

those things that make us feel good! They can be costly so start out with one a month and work your way up to twice a month. I find that I function so much more efficiently when I have one massage a week, so I see it as an investment in myself.

5. Do your best: Start creating excellence within yourself today; right now! I do not care if you are living with your parents and your only goal today was to wash the dishes and clean your room, do the best job you can. Do not do it for an allowance, rather, do it for yourself to prove that you are worthy of being given a task that will display the greatness within you. When you feel you have done a great thing, great feelings of accomplishment follow. Allow these great feelings to keep you motivated, confident, and worry free when new challenges arise.

DAY 17

You are what you think.

Even more important than what we eat, is what we think. Thoughts are just potential things. In my mind I think, "I'm hungry" or "It's almost lunch time" and then a picture pops into my head of a sandwich or other food options. The meal I visualize in my mind brings upon me a feeling of satisfaction, even before I physically receive it. Ultimately, that vision leads me to the kitchen to perform a series of tasks, like toasting the bread, which soon manifests a completed sandwich on my plate. See, the most powerful thing about life is that only YOU have control over how things manifest. Most people do not have a problem fixing a sandwich because we have all fixed one before, so the process of making it is not something we have to waste time convincing ourselves it can be done. A lot of people are their own enemy because they can't even picture how it feels to have accomplished the things they want in life, much less the courage to pursue them.

Today you have an assignment. I want you to travel down your Facebook or Twitter timeline and read the last 20 posts you and your friends posted on YOUR profiles. Your posts are thought in words, so imagine if those things could only fall into a positive, negative, or neutral thought category. Divide them up and if your thoughts have been more negative than positive, imagine the impact you have made on the world as if those thoughts were real things! Now look around and find all the negative things about your life that your negative thoughts are producing and get rid of them. Life is short, and remember, you only have 24 hours in a day. Make each second, word, and thought count to your positive benefit. Ignore others on your timeline who bombard you with negativity; that's the power of the 'delete' button.

DAY 18

The only thing better than winning is preparing to win.

Write down 5 things you made priority over the last year and actually worked your butt off to accomplish. Then, think of all the things you had to do or how hard you had to work to get them done. Now imagine how good it felt when you finally realized you had achieved your goal. No one could tell you a damn thing huh? You felt so proud knowing that no one but YOURSELF put in the time and effort to get things done. If someone had done all the work for you, you wouldn't have appreciated the struggle and you wouldn't have learned much from the experience. The more we learn today, the better we will be able to figure things out in the future. You will beat 90% of your competition by showing up today for something they put off for tomorrow. Show up early, and you beat 5% more of the competition who slept in or showed up late. Show up early and with a plan, then you'll be sure to win 100% of the time!

DAY 19

"In a gentle way, you can shake the world". - Mohandas Gandhi

As an artist, I've always been surrounded by managers or record labels who make it a top priority to make sure I (let's be honest) maintain a big ego. Who wants to listen to a person speak if they have no self confidence right? It gets so easy to get caught up into the spoils of success and all the attention that we almost feel the need to yell even louder hoping to get more attention. I've found that the smallest things I've done in my career thus far have always made the greatest impact. At times I feel the harder I try to force change, the harder it becomes to reach my results. You may not be a millionaire, but look around your life for all the people that would be affected if you weren't here tomorrow. I don't mean to be 'extra gay', but a simple smile, a small email, or poem you share on YouTube may very well touch someone in a country you never even knew existed; that's the magic of the internet! Don't be afraid to use all resources to put yourself out there. Instead of trying to change the world, start with yourself. The people in your home will see the examples you set and begin to follow. Now imagine you have encouraged one person. Later, that one person inspires two more people who turn around and do the same thing to two more people! By one little thing you did, you've already impacted the lives of 7 people. Do the math and before you know it, you've got an army of people following your every move. When you get the attention, it comes before you even notice, so make sure you are doing something positive with it so that positivity can come back to you!

DAY 20

"We all we got!" -Studology101

I've got to dedicate day 20 to 2 individuals who most of you reading this book have all been impacted by whether you will admit it or not. My mission for establishing 6 Colors Entertainment was to show our community that, yes, the world and our families may come against us and have us feeling like our gay family is all we've got, but if we stand together, we are all we need. The year 2012 was definitely a year of growth for the minority owned and urban/hip hop LGBT based business. I don't want to come off in a racial tone when I say this, but never before in history have black owned LGBT been so out spoken and ambitious. However, 2012 was not the start. Anyone who's been gay for the last 5-10 years knows that this is a train that has been moving underground for years but has been foreshadowed by media focused on white markets. From the "L Word" to the Logo channel, all we had to choose from was Bette and Tina fighting, Da Brat rapping, or gay men competing for drag crowns. As of 2012, there has become an urban and worldwide industry for LESBIAN music, reality TV, magazines, books, and non-profit organizations giving us a deeper 'lesbian experience' other than just the night clubs. My vision as of age 23 was to prove that we could create our own markets and be all that "we need". I see others have shared my vision and I am proud of the strides that we as a community have taken. We are all we need to make it happen, but we are just as well all we need to make it fail. It is imperative that we approach our entrepreneurial endeavors with confidence and pride, yet the humility to help each other and remain positive, knowing that there is a bigger picture that we ALL are a part of.

With Studology101 at my 3rd annual "Virgo Bash 2012"

DAY 21

"The day you dream of beating me, wake up and apologize." - Ali

Today, let's have a moment of silence for the competition we've demolished thus far; a day to stroke the ego and re-assure self confidence. If you've reached this point in the book, you've had 3 weeks to set some goals and grow the courage to quench a few victories. Every now and then it's necessary to reflect upon one's accomplishments and 'stroke the ego'. Don't be ashamed to look into the mirror every once in a while to remind yourself that you are the sh*t! Remind yourself today that no matter the test, enemy, circumstance, situation, or goal, it doesn't stand a chance against your will to win and refusal to lose. Remember, there are two types of people in this world; people who complain about the world and people who get up and conquer it! Decide today which person you wish to live as. Get your mind right, get up, and go make it happen!

Closing

Like Kat Williams said, "live your own [damn] life"! Don't waste any more time trying to compare your road to success to someone else's because you'll end up depressed that your life doesn't look like theirs every day. Everyone doesn't need a billion dollars and just because you don't, doesn't make you less of a businesswoman. Everyone isn't meant to be a rapper, model, or actress, so be proud of whatever your passion in life is and spend all your energy trying to be the best at whatever you do. Being wealthy is a state of mind or feeling, not a measure of how good someone's life is. Money is just a measure of numbers and numbers are just a symbol just like a doctor's graduation plaque on the wall. If you feel proud to have accomplished certain things, then let your ability to have control over your life be the motivation to keep making miracles happen. The things and people that money can buy will always come into your life regardless! Ask yourself, how much money does God make every day? Why would God need money! He has the power to speak and make things happen. What's great about being alive is that he/it (or whatever image of 'God' you prefer) made you in his image in order to possess the same power. Be patient, creative, and master the mindset it takes to use that power! I thank you for taking time to read and wish you the best in life! Good luck!...

WEEK 3 ACCOMPLISH LIST

NOTES

All of my albums available for download on I-Tunes.com.

My clothing line available at BillionaireTomBoiSociety.com.

Meet my family!

www.ingramcontent.com/pod-product-compliance
Lightning Source LLC
LaVergne TN
LVHW052258100826
845147LV00001B/80
9780615877396